Christa Nehls

Think A Moment

Thought fragments,
philosophical ideas
and
instructions

Menschin Newsletter 2007-2011

**Volume I of the book series
"Actions speak louder than words"**

© Copyright: Publishing House Menschin

All rights reserved.
Copyright © 2013 by
Publishing House Menschin Christa Nehls
68165 Mannheim, Germany
Translation: Michael Johann Tiefau
Design: selicht, Langenargen

All rights reserved. No part of this publication may be translated, reproduced, stored in a retrieval system, or transmitted, in any form or by any means, electronic, mechanical, photocopying, recording or otherwise, without the prior permission of the publisher.

Printed in Germany.

www.menschin.com

ISBN 978-3-944126-05-0

CONTENTS

Preface to the book series	7
Preface	9
Change	13
Change and Letting go	23
Letting go and Forgiving	33
Reaching Goals	47
Exclusiveness	59
Following New Paths	67
April showers…	75
Actually…	85
Snooker or the New Form of Humility	93
Say so long, but not goodbye…	103
Lifelong Learning	113
Health and Exclusiveness	127
In Conclusion	135
Contact Information	139

Preface to the book series "Actions speak louder than words"

This book in front of you is the first volume of the new series „Actions speak louder than words". It is a compilation of my previous texts that I have published in newsletters. This work literally offers you "moments to think" that are filled with inspiration and creativity for your own first steps towards change in your life.

„Actions speak louder than words" is a book series that guides you from pure thought to action. There are as many instructional books as there is sand on a beach and you will keep reading and reading in these books. The decisive step, however, is missing: action. Every book opens up new possibilities and horizons for you and leads you to new paths. Find the courage of making the decision for yourself to put things into practice. If you do not want to do so, then you have at least enjoyed a good read and made the decision to not make a decision.

Be my guest on my publisher blog and discuss with me. Let me participate because an exchange of ideas with you is important to me.

Many subjects are left in my head and are going to find their way onto paper, into an e-book or an audiobook.

Christa Nehls

November 2011 / February 2013

Preface

Four years ago, I had the idea to write short essays about topics from my work as a counselor. It was and still is important to me to talk about topics that are useful in everyday life. Concerning some texts, I do agree with Martin Luther who is supposed to have said in Worms, Germany: „Here I stand, I can do no other. May God help me, amen!" (Yes, I was at the monument and it is engraved there exactly like this in German.) Unfortunately, the historical records say something different: "Thus, I cannot and will not recant anything, for going against conscience is neither right nor safe. May God help me, amen!" As you may have already noticed, I am rather pedantic from time to time. When such pedantic moments occur, I would rather like to be precise than imperfect.

Time and time again, I have received feedback on my plea about health, but also on the topic of saying goodbye, for example. I present my take on each subject in every text, of course, but my personal involvement in these two texts seems to be so profound that I have touched my readership in a very special way – my way.

Let us take a closer look: Saying goodbye is a difficult topic in our society. Especially death is an essential part of it. We try to avoid it; we try to keep it out of sight during our lives, yet we have been carrying it with us since the day we were born. Death, sickness and infirmity, poverty and unemployment, disfigurement and ugliness – all these things are overlooked by us; we do not want to have anything to do with them and we do not want to be confronted with them.

These are exactly the reasons why I am intrigued by these topics, why they interest me and why they spur me to think and to ask questions. I also want to say something, want to put a spotlight on something and form my own opinion; I want to provoke gently or I simply want to encourage others or make a plea.

Our health care system suffers from its members' demands, their expectations and their pronounced desire for service without taking responsibility for themselves, as in: "Just take care of it, doc." It also suffers from the unwillingness of people to catch up on things and learn. Moreover, our health care system supports exactly these trends. Having informed and enlightened patients is undesirable – even if it be just because such patients are exhausting. Many courageous steps have to be taken here. With my plea for holistic medicine, I express my annoyance of the polarization between classical and alternative medicine. The latter does not even exist; all methods of treatment supplement each other and are therefore complementary, not alternative. We also have to get an understanding of which way of thinking and cultural area gave rise to a method of treatment.

Regarding this topic, Sabine Kubitz wrote to me: "That's the only way to go. How can we expect the TCM, for example, to have a lasting positive effect if we, at the same time, don't know anything about its philosophy? As long as I, as a patient, am waiting to be cured by someone or something, it's not going to work at all in the long run!"

Sabine is exactly right: We have to take responsibility for ourselves as well as our actions and bear the consequences. This is the only way for us to change something, to shape our future actively and to live instead of being lived.

NB: My cooperation partner Ingrid Lardon has dedicated herself to the subject of trauma therapy. She has been a qigong trainer (SKA) for quite some time now. For me, the most exciting thing about this is her method of connecting both areas in order to offer her clients a piece of oneness by means of physical experience, among other things. The more I see and hear, the more information I gather – for example about a pain therapist who links classical medicine with naturopathic medicine, listening, herbal compresses and many other things. His patients achieve a higher quality of life more quickly.

So what has brought me to the decision to compile my newsletters in a book? The idea to let my clients get to know me better and to convey my ways of working and thinking on the one hand, and to offer the texts in a more handy form on the other hand. You probably know this situation as well, a small book or paperback, respectively, is more convenient to handle than several US Letter sheets and you can easily carry it with you in your bag.

My readers have encouraged me with their e-mails to continue writing. Here are some examples:

"Great, a new newsletter arrived today. I have already printed it and I am looking forward to reading it in bed tonight while comfortably drinking a cup of tea."

Or almost in an amusing way:

"I always print the newsletter out and put it to the other reading material in the guest toilet. The only thing that is obviously read over and over again are the newsletters. They are always quite tattered."

I am always happy to get such messages as they show me that I have my finger on the pulse of the times and that I satisfy the needs of my readership.

Christa Nehls

September 23, 2011

Change

People change during the course of their lives…

At the time when the Digital Equipment Corporation (DEC) was acquired by Compaq in 1998, a management colleague from the USA wrote the following words:

We never know exactly,
if something will improve, when we change it.
We sure do know,
that we have to change, if we want to improve.

The news just keep coming in at my desk these days. Every single one of them has something to do with (the courage for) change:

- Friends are going to Africa as aid workers
- The standard meter is being discussed (see also the GEO magazine issue of March 2008) and is to be replaced by more modern methods of measurement.
- A big project is canceled
- Help me, I am gaining weight! How can I keep my weight stable?
- Volunteers complain about their colleague's unwillingness to take responsibility for themselves

Change means letting go. Letting go means giving your place to someone or something else. Abandoning something is something different, it means harm or destruction, among other things. Change in one's life always means putting aside old habits one has grown fond of and embracing the new wholeheartedly. [1]

But what does this mean for my friends in Africa? They have left the European culture with a lot of courage and commitment, they let go of the culture that is strongly shaped by measurable performance and time measurement. A new culture has welcomed them. This culture has time, there are no appointments that need to be chased after. The performance requirements and pressure are nowhere to be found, either. Thus, it is important, first of all, to get to know the people, the culture, the customs and the country itself. Time is abundant. The primary goal is to embrace the new and the unknown. Only with empty hands can you reach for the new.

And the standard meter... what does this have to do with change? Until now, there has been a piece of metal in a maximum security safe near Paris. This safe is opened every few years in order to check whether the standard meter is still there and whether it still has the correct weight.

---

[1] Alfred Adler, founder of the school of individual psychology, said: "The past is only good for learning from it and then forgetting everything again ... and ... if we did not sleep, thus everything that we have experienced, seen, learned and discovered would remain in our memory. Our memory would be overloaded. Since we all sleep, we forget a lot."

Apart from the standard meter, there are six further base units of measurement, by the way. Efforts are currently being made to replace and redefine these units of measurement. Scientists are passionately and nitpickingly discussing, with extremely high standards that need to be met, what degree of accuracy the evidence has to reach before the new definition is finally accepted.

You can look it up in further detail in the 3/2008 GEO magazine issue. The matter is still undecided.

A big voluntary project was built from scratch by a few committed people that nourished this project with their lifeblood, but it still fails gloriously. It fails because of a lack of money and commitment. How could this happen? Well, the project did not have enough time to grow, just like every single thing in nature needs time to flourish. Consequently, it came to be that the political bodies and institutions were taken by surprise by the idea and the sponsors rejected us because of the lack of recommendations and successes. In addition, there was a too low demand for what this project was offering. Where was the change here, then? In this case, the change can be found at the end. The wasted lifeblood acted like a lot of glue, it was very hard to let go. Only when the source of bliss became a burden did the volunteers give way to change and let it go.

Help me, I am gaining weight! How can I keep my weight stable? You might ask, "What does this have to do with change?" Losing weight is fast and easy. Counting calories, points and so on is child's play. It is keeping your weight stable that is the hard part. Who has not already heard of the yo-yo effect? Long-term programs seem to solve the problem here, don't they? Sure, if already pose this rhetorical question – they are no problem solvers, either. They will not work as long as the participant is waiting for the problem to be solved instead of actively solving it himself or herself. Counting calories is not the issue here.

It is much more important to understand that keeping your weight stable has something to do with exercise, stamina and the will to change old habits that are stuck in the routine of everyday life. All this, including drawing conclusions from it and keeping it up afterwards, is going to do the trick. But if the old habits are stronger than the will to keep your weight on a lower level, then the yo-yo effect has already started.

In this case, it is of no use that new clothes that still fitted so perfectly just a few weeks ago are hanging in the closet. It is of no use to moan, to frustrate yourself and to complain: "Why am I unable to do it while others are able? Why have I put on weight even though I eat so less? Other people eat so much and yet they stay thin." There is only one thing one can do here: taking yourself seriously, becoming your own center of attention, appreciating yourself, taking care of yourself (and your health etc.), following that new path unswervingly and staying true to yourself as well as your own needs.

Only if you gradually tear down your own habits can you build up your ideal weight. What are these old habits? The job is more important, the family is more important, the children's and friends' worries are more important etc. The new eating habits as well as the planning of the preparation and the regularity fall by the wayside. But what about the people that have put on too much weight? Well, they get their yo-yo and therefore their protective shell back. So only the willingness for change, real change, is going to solve the problem.

Similar applies to pain patients. I have gotten to know many pain patients my life, especially since 1997. Since then, I have become one myself, by the way. I have talked to many, especially to those who have found a way of living with the pain or banishing it from their lives. They are different from those people who "love" their pain. They have made the decision to take their lives into their own hands and to take care of themselves. They have made their own decision not to love the sickness anymore. They look out for what is good for them, set limits to what their fellow human beings are doing to them and they do not let themselves be sucked dry by energy vampires anymore.

There certainly are pain patients who suffer from chronic pain due to a severe accident or a physical illness. Interestingly, these people also experience a greater fulfillment in their lives as soon as they decide to choose themselves rather than the pain. This new way of treating themselves helps them to handle the sickness differently and to reevaluate the importance of that sickness in their lives. The pain is still present, it is just not permanently in the foreground anymore.

Over the last few days, I heard many voluntary workers (especially speakers of self-help groups) complain about their members being in a constant state of expectation and demanding more and more from them. According to them, the participation and contribution of their members is either very low or nonexistent. Being a speaker of a self-help group, I can certainly sympathize with that because I have made the same experience. Of course we could let ourselves be overcome by complaints and laments now. But none of these active members do that. Instead, we let bygones be bygones and look towards the future. In this future, the active members could meet and continue working committed beyond the limits of a specially oriented group, invite speakers, organize events together and do much more. There are already eight people! This is the change and the courage to look to the future and to take action.

The result: the knowledge that the new path looks confusing and irritating to their surroundings is what they all have in common. If you follow a new path – with whatever goal in mind – remember to take your fellow human beings with you and to keep them up-to-date about what is happening.

„I cannot change others, only myself.
But if I change myself, almost everything around me changes with me." (from the school of individual psychology)

So if we have made the decision to change, the next step follows: action. It gets serious now. As I have already mentioned numerous times previously, it becomes difficult at exactly that moment when you have been left on your own. The old habits return with all their might. That is the reason, why it is so important, for every single one of us, to develop strategies for self-motivation and perseverance early on.

The old habits were comfortable because they were familiar. No matter how bad they were or how much mental pressure they have caused, they are familiar. They tempt us, they call us, they pull and seduce us. They know exactly how difficult it is to follow this new path since it is unfamiliar. Thus, the old habits are like sirens with their beguiling song. Break free from this cycle of old habits. Take full advantage of spring for new experiences. Believe in your own strengths and abilities. You are stronger than you think.

Sogyal Rinpoche, a Buddhist scholar, once said: "Just like the rocks that do not shatter when the waves pound the coast, but are polished into beautiful shapes, so can our character be shaped and our hard edges be smoothed."

Change and Letting go

Stages
by Hermann Hesse

As every flower withers and all youth ends,
So does every stage of life, every wisdom
And every virtue bloom in its due time,
And cannot last forever.
'Tis the heart that, at every call of life,
Needs to depart and start anew for forming new
and unknown bonds
Undauntedly and without mourning.
And in every new beginning dwells a spell
Which wards us, and guides our way of living.
With high spirits we shall pass age after age,
Yet not cling to one as to our home,
The world's spirit neither binds nor limits,
But wants to heave and enrich us, stage by stage.
Scarce are we set in one of life's spheres,
Accustomed to convenience, indolence is here.
Only by voyage and starting something new
May convenience be defeated, long overdue.
Maybe even in our last hours
Can we be led to new realms and young flowers.
Calling us, of which life will never grow weary…
So take leave, heart, and be well, not dreary!

At the time when the Digital Equipment Corporation (DEC) was acquired by Compaq in 1998, a management colleague from the USA wrote the following words:

We never know exactly,

if something will improve, when we change it.

We sure do know,

that we have to change, if we want to improve.

No, no, it is not what you think it is. This has nothing to do with me being a scatterbrain, my vanishing thinking abilities or something of that sort. This is a new issue of my newsletter. I am taking the liberty of picking up the subject of the last newsletter and elaborating it further, just as it is the custom in music. (Nb: On the basis of this example, you can see that I, too, feel still attached to some things and cannot let go of them quite yet.) Changes have a lot to do with letting go. Another reference to the previous chapter: "Only with empty hands can you reach for the new." Sounds plausible, doesn't it? An example from practice: You are cleaning up your apartment. Both of your hands are full with all kinds of things that you want to move to a different spot (or that you want to throw in the trash); then another thing enters your field of vision, you reach for it and your hands are empty all of a sudden. Everything has fallen to the ground and has been damaged to a greater or lesser degree. Admittedly, this happened involuntarily.

You are upset. All of this just because you have forgotten that your hands were already full due to all that holding tight. We experience exactly the same thing with everything else that we absolutely want to hold tight, as the following incomplete list illustrates:

- Property
- People, e.g. children, parents
- Thoughts
- Situations
- Work
- Partner(ship)
- Victimhood
- Events
- Timetables
- Behavioral patterns
- and many other things...

You may also continue this list and be creative.

What does letting go mean?

From a linguistic point of view, it consists of two words: "let" and "go". During the last couple of years, I have interviewed many people about the meaning this phrase has for them, especially with regard to people. Most of them said it had something to do with "abandoning something", "throwing something away", "not wanting something anymore", "rejecting something". Exceedingly few said "leaving something as it is" or "the lack of a reason to change something". That is interesting because we are thus returning to the example of "cleaning up" that was mentioned above.

Things fall out of our hands because we are already holding other things tight. How much easier things would be if we did not hold anything tight. There would be the chance of reaching for everything without letting anything fall down. So only with empty hands can you reach for the new.

What does it mean when we hold tight instead of let go?

Deep down within us is the fear to be alone, to do something alone and to be responsible alone. In that case, the better and easier alternative seems to be to cling to the old and customary ways of doing things. A usual hell is better than an unknown heaven. You remember, "We never know exactly, if something will improve, when we change it." For me, the important realization lies here; we look for security in the familiar things. This prohibits us from letting go, it prohibits us from exploring the new heavens. We are afraid of the new and the unknown. It means insecurity.

An example: A mother and her child are on the playground. The child absolutely wants to get on the slide alone. The mother is afraid, accompanies the child and holds its hand while it slides down. The child whines the entire time, it wants to slide on its own. Both do not get any joy out of this affair. It would have been nice if the mother had had the courage of letting her child go and letting it gain some experience on its own. Thus, she guarded her child and protected it. This does not bring the child any advantages during its later life. It rather learns anxiety than courage in this case.

Fathers are more relaxed regarding these situations: they leave their children the necessary space to explore the world. Even though they do have a watchful eye on them from a "distance" if any possible kind of emergency should still come up, they mainly convey to the child: "I trust you and I have confidence in your capabilities."

As Erik Blumenthal writes in "The new ways to inner freedom" [1]: "The new often means transformation, and this means dying and coming into existence again. The old has to die in order to make room for the new. [...] Most of the time the new indicates a mistake in the old. However, nobody likes to admit a mistake, is willing to change his current attitude towards life or even to change the direction completely. The old is perceived as an anchor, as a rope to which one can hold on, as security. The new, in contrast to this, often causes insecurity. One has built up his world, is accustomed to it, and is therefore inclined to stay there due to convenience and the sluggishness of the heart and the spirit. [...] Moreover, the spiritually new requires a new thinking."

---

[1] Ger. orig.: Blumenthal, Erik; Neue Wege zur inneren Freiheit, Horizonte Verlag

Change as a solution and the belief in yourself

Therefore, it follows that we have to change habits. We have the freedom to do this and so it depends on every single one individually. Another quote from Blumenthal: "The term of freedom. [...] The outer freedom becomes important on the human level. This outer freedom, however, needs to be restricted for the coexistence of humans because one human can only have so much outer freedom inasmuch as he does not infringe the freedom of another fellow human being with it. On the spiritual level [...] the inner freedom is essential, and this inner freedom is unlimited."

However, there are also rules that need to be observed in the outer world: traffic rules, for example. We cannot suddenly drive on a one-way street heading in the wrong direction. Blumenthal continues: "A human makes use of his inner freedom when he no longer perceives the traffic regulations as a 'must', but when he, in his inner freedom, rather makes the decision to want that which he ought to want, namely, to observe the traffic rules that benefit everybody."

Alright, now we have reached the crucial point: It is absolutely important that we believe in ourselves and our judgment, that we free ourselves from information and opinions that were (and still are) conveyed to us by others – family, friends, teachers, educators, the press, the media etc. If we allow ourselves to think for ourselves, if we allow ourselves to act as we think best, then we have the chance of rearranging our lives, of letting go of the old and getting the new. This also includes giving other people in our lives the space they need, giving them the opportunity of autonomous development and a life of their own instead of imprisoning them by means of holding them tight, i.e. (over)caution, protecton and (parental) care.

In support for our actions we still require some optimism, acceptance and solution orientation. Then we will soon come to a point where we are able to leave victimhood behind, take responsibility for ourselves and our actions, establish relationships (networking) and shape the future ourselves.

If we stop
- evaluating our self-esteem from the approval and words of others,
- defining ourselves through others,

then we will find the courage to follow own and new paths.

If we take responsibility for ourselves and our actions, then we will have the courage to follow new paths.

These paths are new, which means that we are cautious and insecure at first. But after a certain amount of time, we become more daring, we explore the path more and more briskly and thus we continually practice the exploration and living of new things. At the same time, we increasingly let go of the old, we are able to leave the past the way it was because we know that it cannot be changed anymore. The future lies ahead of us, we can influence and shape it. The only prerequisite for this is to say:

"Yes, I do. Yes, I will take my life into my own hands. Yes, I will shape my life. Yes, I will leave victimhood behind. Yes, I will take responsibility for myself."

Oh, you have already heard of all of this, you already knew that? I have not told you anything new? Knowledge is good, but the action is the decisive part. Well, the more you already know, the better. So let's start changing. DO something!

Regarding this topic, George Bernard Shaw said: "I don't believe in circumstances. The people who get on in this world are the people who get up and look for the circumstances they want, and, if they can't find them, make them." Furthermore, Luise Rinser said: „One does not even need to know what new things are to come, one just has to be ready and confident."

Letting go and Forgiving

Quite some time ago, someone gave me a stone with the remark: "For letting go." It looked matte and was/is dark blue, medium blue and black. Such an inconspicuous stone for letting go. Very well, then.

As I like minerals very much, I looked up its difficult name 'dumortierite' and found out that it was first described in the 19th century (so Saint Hildegard of Bingen did not know about it!). It was named after the French paleontologist Eugène Dumortier. The stone forms in magma that contains a lot of silicic acid and it can be found between Madagascar and South Africa. Being a ceramic raw material for the industry, it is used for the manufacture of insulators and laboratory equipment. The material can only be worked with difficulty and counterfeiting it is impossible. So far so good. The natural scientist in me was satisfied.

In the end, every stone is a marvel of nature. How accurate and true the ascribed healing properties are is beyond my knowledge. From a psychological point of view, I am okay with "taking" something in order to remind oneself of specific intentions or actions. That is just the same as tying a string around one's finger as a reminder.

Why am I telling you this? Well, this stone is also called the "take-it-easy stone" and it is supposed to give its owner courage and confidence in difficult situations. At least this stone now reminds me of "taking it easy" and "letting it go"; it reminds me of not "bearing grudges". Furthermore, it reminds me of "Don't make such a fuss about it!"

This "take-it-easy" attitude seems to be missing in our society, or where else would this enormous striving towards a hedonistic society come from?

A couple of days ago I read the following sentence: "Forgiving gives me inner peace."

What does "forgiving" mean?

Where does this word come from? It consists of two parts. On the one hand there is "give", which obviously means "to give (something)". The prefix "for", on the other hand, means "away" or "completely". What exactly, in a more modern sense of the phrase, has to be "given away completely"? One's offenses and/or accusations. So "to forgive" means "to give up one's offenses / accusations". But who is being accused? Someone who is guilty and who has burdened himself or herself with guilt, at least in court. When I do not forgive someone, I will keep that guilt in mind and will always bear it with me in form of a grudge. I bear a grudge against someone.

Let us also look at the phrase "bearing a grudge"

If I do not want to forgive someone, I keep my accusation up. This accusation will remain in my head and in my thoughts. I will bear it as a grudge. Who is bearing the burden here? Certainly the accuser, the person who cannot forgive and still wants to accuse. So it is I. I have my cross to bear, not the person I cannot forgive. In the worst case scenario, the other person cannot even remember anymore the event or the reason, why I am bearing a grudge. Yet I have the burden to bear. My hands are full and thus I am unable to reach for the new or to even touch anything new.

Bearing a grudge

In what kinds of situations do we, for example, bear a grudge and do not forgive?

- the partner has left me / has broken up with me/was unfaithful; he possibly even left without any explanation
- the child has broken something (valuable)
- my mother did not trust me when I was little
- my parents did not love me
- someone has left / died without saying goodbye to me
- my superior has denied me the raise
- that guy snatched the last parking lot away from me
- and much more

Oh, what grudges do we bear against other people! Let us take a closer look. Every single one of these scenarios has something to do with hurt, offense and disrespectfulness towards me or us, correct? Inner tensions are the result of this. The statement "forgiving gives me inner peace" is still left unanswered. Let us think a step further. Maybe the following questions will help us on our way towards forgiving:

- Does that particular person actually know that I feel hurt by him or her?
- Maybe he or she perceived that which was hurtful to me in a fundamentally different way?
- Of what use can bearing a grudge against that person be in that moment?
- Do I myself gain a benefit or a profit from me being unwilling to forget?
- What do I gain from not letting go?
- What profit do I make?
- And what price do I pay… apart from me continuing to bear the burden and apart from good portions of my brain being fully engaged in the task of continued grudge-bearing?

Would it be not much simpler, and possibly also nicer, to be free from this burden and to invest energy in new and nice things for me? Maybe you remember me writing the following a couple of letters previously: "Only with empty hands can you reach for the new." As long as I am holding a grudge against someone, my hands will be full.

This is something new and you have not already heard of it? Regarding this topic, André Gide once said: "One doesn't discover new lands without consenting to lose sight, for a very long time, of the shore." For him, letting go is the prerequisite for everything else. That is exactly how it is with bearing a grudge. If my hands are completely full, I am no longer free in my actions. Full hands restrain me from doing actions, actions such as forgiving and therefore making a friend and reaching something new.

Now the time has come for me to decide what I want: bearing a grudge or letting go, full hands or empty hands. What price am I willing to pay for gaining what kind of profit? If the price I pay for bearing a grudge is too high in comparison with the profit I gain from it, then it is high time for me to get started!

Forgive others as well as yourself. Especially forgive yourself, over and over again. Many people tell me that they have already forgiven some people during the course of their lives. When I ask them whether they have also forgiven themselves some things from time to time, I receive tears, hot and sad tears most of the time.

Nb: Right now, you are probably wondering about me writing: "…being unwilling to forget". And you are doing this justifiably so. In the school of individual psychology, we say: "Oh, you're saying that you can't do this. Please be honest, you don't want to do this." We trust people to have the necessary skills and capabilities.

The children's view

Let us be inspired. During class, children had the task of brainstorming what forgiving means.
(Taken from: "Texte lesen und verstehen" ("Reading and understanding texts"), Barcz & Szpadzik, Poland)

They gathered the following responses:
- ending a conflict/an argument
- no more arguing
- apologizing
- agreeing with someone
- pardoning
- begging someone's pardon
- making a friend

...and this, furthermore, became...
- People often are hurt so deeply that they cannot forget it.
- Some people do not want to forgive although they would feel better if they did.
- Forgiving does not mean that one is weak; it means that one frees himself.
- Forgiving can be practiced – at first with lighter offenses.
- It helps to write our feelings to the person that hurt us. If you do this, it is not important to actually send this letter.

Burning it, burying it, tearing it apart or simply putting it aside are often better ways of handling it, else this method could lead to vengeance and that is not the purpose of it.
- One should under no circumstances cling to his or her anger. Forgiving does not need any confrontation.
- It is important to look at the past events from a different point of view – this teaches tolerance.
- Meditation and prayer help us being able to forgive.
- Forgiving is not the same as forgetting.

By closely examining these statements, we can say the following: If we take responsibility for ourselves as well as our actions, then we have the courage of following new paths; then we are free in our decisions and actions. "New paths" also contains the meaning of discovering new perspectives for oneself and staying with oneself. Maybe you remember previous texts written by me in which I quoted Dreikurs: "We cannot change others, only ourselves. But if we change ourselves, almost everything around us changes with us." Evidence has been brought forward recently which indicates that this saying is actually older and by someone else.

The children have realized something: it is not easy to forgive. It takes some time, it requires some work and even more personal responsibility. Furthermore, the most significant realization is: forgiving means that one is strong and frees himself or herself. And yet these children have realized the most crucial fact: Forgiving is possible if we want it.

What forgiving is not

Another very important point: Concerning forgiving, a nice person once said to me in an almost insulted manner: "But then I am the idiot, I give in, I am the one who backs down in such a situation. What about my feelings?" No, that has nothing to do with forgiving. This is the struggle for power, the retaining of a position of power, the keeping of the moral high ground while I already feel inferior otherwise.

An example as thinking aid

I will give you an example that certainly seems very familiar to you: A child goes to school and does its best there. The grades, however, are rather average. But it keeps on studying and it understands most of what it learns in school. The child returns home with his grades. Upon arrival, it is met with questions like: "Which grades do the others have? What? They have better grades than you? Why don't you know how to do this? Are you too stupid for this?" The child is sad, disappointed and downcast in the truest sense of the word. All this despite its trying hard and doing everything that is possible. The child gets older and becomes adult. It secretly accuses its parents of having discouraged it and not having had confidence in it. It silently suffers. It bears a grudge against them and, consequently, its heart is filled with it and its hands are full. Thus, it keeps its position on the moral high ground as well as a view that is full of if's, could's and might-have-been's.

What else could this adult with this small, disappointed, and grudge-bearing child in him or her do? He or she could take a different perspective, for example. How could this be achieved? By understanding that the parents are also only human and that they always did the best they could do during every moment of their lives. If you are a parent yourself, then this is the most beautiful relief you can get from your children in your life. We all are children, children in an aging skin. When we have become adults, we tell the child within us how to forgive and let go. By the way: the child within us likes to learn, it is curious.

Taking responsibility for one's life

Let us take another look at the realizations of the children in school mentioned previously. During the course of our lives we apparently forget how to forgive. Why else should we think of so many things as un-for-giv-able? How many times do we humans have to endure being hurt and offended that we bear so many grudges? Maybe Nietzsche was right when he said: "What child wouldn't have any reason to cry due to its parents." Anselm Grün has a response to that: "Whether we find our own course of life or let ourselves be determined by our life story depends on the way our parental wounds heal." [2]

---

[2] Anselm Grün, Das kleine Buch vom wahren Glück ("The little book of true happiness") © September 2008

This seems to be the key aspect here.

If we take the responsibility for our own life, then we no longer need authority figures such as parents anymore. In order to achieve this, we need the ability of understanding and recognizing our thoughts and feelings. Forgiving takes pressure from our own lives and alleviates them and therefore new energy for the shaping of our lives is released by it – only when we understand this do we finally take the responsibility for our lives, our thinking, our feelings and our actions.

The stone – the dumortierite – still lies in front of me while I am writing this. It has carried me through these lines that, to be honest, have not been easy for me this time. So the stone reminded me to take it easy. Keep the twinkle in your eyes and don't be so serious about everything, then you will also find it easy (or easier) to forgive.

Fragments gathered from the Internet (wikiquote) about „forgiving"

"All mistakes that one makes are more pardonable than the measures taken to hide them."

François de La Rochefoucauld, Maximes supprimées ("Deleted maxims")

"Overlook much in others, nothing in yourself!"

Cleobulus of Lindos according to Ausonius, Sayings of the Seven Sages

"Admitting one's guilt and forgiving are the two highest mountain ranges that we often have to climb laboriously during our lives."

Ernst Ferstl, Lebensspuren ("Tracks of life")

"Mistakes that children were taught by their parents are the least likely mistakes to be forgiven by these parents."

Marie von Ebner-Eschenbach, Aphorismen ("Aphorisms"), Reclam Verlag, Stuttgart, 2002, p. 11

"God does not forgive what humans forgive. Humans do not forgive what God forgives."

Franz Werfel, Zwischen Oben und Unten ("Between above and below")

"I beg your pardon. This is just a natural human affair. – This is just a formal question – I do – I do love all – all people! I do love, I am committed to doing it!"

Erich Mielke

"One always mistakes when one does not close his eyes for forgiving or recognizing himself."

Maurice Maeterlinck, Pelléas et Mélisande ("Pelléas and Mélisande")

"My best friend even forgives me for the truth."

Billy, Wir Kleindenker, p. 195

"Forgive the confessor!"

Tibullus, Elegies I, VI, 29

"Forgiving is the best revenge."

Proverb

Reaching Goals

At the turn of every year, the New Year's resolutions spring up like mushrooms. During this year, I have already given some talks about this topic and have discussed the following question with the listeners: "How do I keep my New Year's resolutions?"

Nine out of ten New Year's resolutions have been forgotten or have failed three weeks after the start of the new year. What is the reason for that? This was the most essential question.

Well, what is it? Let us look for it together: How do most of the New Year's resolutions look like? They are made according to the following pattern:

- "From now on, I'm not going to do this or that anymore"
- "I'm going to change my behavior / way of living"
- "I'm not going to do… ever again."

Does this look familiar? The New Year's resolution, finally. You are also proud of finally addressing exactly this issue. For our thinking, these resolutions seem great and terrific. If we use the phrasing mentioned above, many things sound very decisive and specific. It is definitely going to work. It is going to be different this time. We have an exact plan of what needs to be done in our heads…

And then there is our subconscious. Now it is standing there and has no idea what is going on. Just to be perfectly clear, more than 90% of our brain has no idea what is going on. What was seemingly phrased and postulated so clearly is actually completely incomprehensible to the poor subconscious. There are problems of communication! What now? Herein lies the problem and failure of the resolutions.

Furthermore, frustration, disappointment and self-reproaches are added to the mix. We accuse ourselves of being losers and slouches; eventually, we will not even dare to do the simplest things anymore. We are inept.

At least at his point, it is time to consciously look at the situation and ask the following questions:

- What is my goal? Is it really my goal?
- How do I formulate this goal?
- What steps / intervals towards the goal are appropriate for me?
- How do I reward myself for intermediate goals?
- Do I have multiple goals and are all of them equally important?
- Can I achieve all goals simultaneously or do I arrange them in a specific order? How should I do that?
- Does it make sense to make detours for reaching this goal?
- What hindrances / obstacles / impediments are there?
- Is the goal even in my reach? Do I need comrades and supporters for it?
- Am I doing everything right or am I making a fool of myself forever?

I encounter the most interesting variants in my practical work as a counselor.

"I want to change my life, it cannot go on like this. Everything has to become easier."

This resolution is destined to fail right from the start because this goal is unspecific. Even if that particular person knows its current life and says that it cannot go on like this, this does neither help our subconscious nor our way of living. This is no goal, this is a vague wisp of nothing. Here, the first step is specifying the goal, e.g. I do not give my adult children money anymore, but rather a gas coupon, I am thus setting limits and keeping them. Yes, sure, I can already hear the objection that this already was an intermediate goal. Well, it is indeed a goal, but not an intermediate one on the way to the big main goal. Goals are always specific and they can be planned and prepared in advance. Wishes, on the other hand, are rather unspecific / in-tang-ible and they may come true or may not come true. Do you notice the difference?

Let us also look at the language: expressions like "I hope", "I wish", "I will", "I want to" lead to hoping, wishing, willing and wanting. Expressions such as "Every Tuesday at eight o'clock, I go to the gym", "I'm immediately going to write a list of all my activities that still need to be done" or "I'm going to make an appointment with XY and call them right now." Sentences like these directly lead to action, to doing something. As you have noticed, actions are clearly and precisely phrased without the help of any linguistic fillers or modal verbs that leave a lot of room for interpretation of and deviation from the plan. It is also advisable to incorporate an exact point in time in these sentences.

It is extremely important to distinguish whether I pursue a specific goal or a wish, or as HPZ (www.hpz.com) puts it: "a wishy". Every goal has a different size. Depending on its size, I can reach the goal in a couple of days, in a month, in a quarter of a year, in one year or in multiple years. The bigger a goal is, the more important it is to divide it into different steps. A path consists of many steps. Most people still take the first step, but then it turns out, that doing it, is actually harder and more laborious than previously thought and the time runs short. Everything runs short – apart from the excuses. Maybe it was not their goal after all and they were afraid of making a fool of themselves.

You probably have been nodding the entire time. I am sure that all of you are familiar with this.

Do you want to change something? Then you should even plan the small goals in advance: Schedule a date by which you want to have reached the goal. Now the intermediate steps come into play. Do you need any? If so, what kind of steps are they and what are their respective dates? Create a project plan. For your private life, this seems laborious and thus superfluous. Many enough resolutions also fail in business life. I often get to hear "Oh, I will remember that, I don't need to write that down." And then the drama as well as the excuses begin. Furthermore, making this goal public (i.e. telling someone or many about it) is also important.

Yes, there it is again – the fear of making a fool of oneself, the fear of failing. We will return to this fear later. Now only one thing is important: Stay courageous and keep hanging on, even if you are afraid. You grow along with your successes as well as your failures. Successes are made up of a chain of previous failures. Not that I want to convince you of failures, but failures are just a regular part of the bigger picture, just like light and darkness, heaven and hell, water and earth. Every thing has two sides, just like a coin.

Let us continue: What events could occur that prevent me from reaching my goal? How do I handle them when they occur? Have enough alternatives up your sleeve and keep the most important one in mind: spontaneity and serenity. Just let the things come, it could be that an unexpected alternative comes up that you had never thought of before. This alternative could even help you skip a couple of steps and therefore accelerate the reaching of the goal.

Oh, and here comes the first and biggest obstacle: quickening, haste, rapidness, speed, lack of patience and lack of stamina. Everything right now and immediately. The main topic of our time.

The reaching of goals takes time, patience and stamina. Have the courage for your very own personal pace for reaching your goal. There are detours available sometimes. Detours are considered to be a loss as well as a waste of time in our cultural and collective thinking. Let us at least once look at detours a little differently: detours increase your local knowledge. Do you know how many tries (or detours) Edison needed to get a fully functional lightbulb? About 4,000. Moreover, he always said „I am grateful for knowing about 4,000 ways how not to produce a lightbulb." He had stamina, patience, took his time and learned incredibly much during the development stage. He was not afraid of making a fool of himself. He was absolutely and thoroughly convinced to be on the right path. We can learn from that. It is an inexhaustible example for the reaching of goals. Never lose heart.

Furthermore, always have the courage to adjust your goal. Long-term goals in particular are under the influence of a kind of zeitgeist. Let's say you want to make your house energy efficient during the next ten years, for example. Research discovers new possibilities all the time. Maybe it is not yet possible to install solar collectors on your roof because it points towards the East and the angle of your roof does not allow an installation. But in four years time, the solar technology will be advanced enough so that you can also install solar collectors on the North side of your roof. Who knows? Please also take the aspects of modernization and updating into account when examining your goals. This has something to do with strength and self-consciousness.

Disgrace and Embarrassment

Several days ago, a reader (Inge Delarber, Mackenbach, Germany) wrote in the newspaper:

All people can write two books. Book 1: My mistakes, book 2: The mistakes of others. We are afraid of failing, we are afraid of making a fool out of ourselves. "How embarrassing!", we say to ourselves when we fail at something. „Hopefully nobody has noticed that." A new approach helps here as well: the courage for incompleteness. Mistakes help us. They help us realize that we are currently following the wrong path. If we take a closer look, we understand what we have lacked and therefore why we have done this mistake. We learn from it, new things emerge from it. We become creative here because we take our time to examine it. So is it still so bad to make mistakes, to fail, to be human?

And while we are already on the subject: it also helps to ask people for their support. So many things are so much easier when they are done together – including the reaching of goals.

This is the courage for incompleteness: admitting that I do not have enough strength to reach a goal on my own.

One of the questions listed above is still unanswered: I have multiple goals. Which one is important and how do I arrange them in the right order? First of all, I check whether some goals are only reachable if I have reached other goals from my list first.

I can find that out fairly quickly. After that, I have two possibilities of arranging the rest of the goals in the right order. On the one hand I use the Eisenhower method. Caution: I need a lot of courage and decisiveness for this.

Eisenhower divided his tasks into

IMPORTANT / URGENT / NOT IMPORTANT / NOT URGENT.

We can express it as a chart:

	URGENT	NOT URGENT
IMPORTANT	A	B
NOT IMPORTANT	C	G

G – garbage bin; small talk, rumor mill, diversions

A – It is urgent and important, e.g. resolving conflicts,

B – it is important and not urgent, e.g. doing networking,

C – phone calls, (unexpected) visits, e-mails, mail

Also take a look at the Seminarschmiede ("seminary smithy") (www.seminarhaus-schmiede.de/pdf/prioritaeten.pdf) and see what they have to offer. You can read an interesting presentation there called "Am I doing things right or am I doing the right things?"

By going through their lists according to this method, some clients try to tell me that everything belonged to category A. Thus, the first step towards burning out is made. Everything is important, everything is urgent, nothing can be left unattended. In this case, a different method called "pairwise comparison" can help. Suppose you have five goals that all seem equally important and urgent to you. You also know that reaching all of them simultaneously is impossible.

You definitely need a priority list. In the following paragraphs, I am going to describe the simplest version of the pairwise comparison to you:

Take the goal you wrote down first on your list. Now compare this goal with the one that you wrote down second. Which goal is more important to you? Check the more important one off. After that, compare the first with the third one, then the first with the fourth and the first with the fifth one. Then take the second goal on your list and compare it with the third, the second with the fourth and the second with the fifth. Proceed likewise with the third and the fourth goal. The fifth goal does not have any further partner. This method can be expanded according to your own discretion. Most of the time it stops to be useful after 10 or 11 goals. You now have a "best of" list of your activities. Most of the checks are now next to the topic with the highest priority. As it is in first place, you do it first, …and so on.

If this seems too trivial to you (but not to your subconscious), then you can refine this procedure a little further. Instead of just deciding "either or", you can also choose the following variation:

Let us suppose the pair consists of X and Y. Then you decide during comparison that X is more important than Y and X receives two points; if Y is more important than X, then Y receives two points; if both are equally important, then both receive one point each. In my very personal opinion, you do not want to decide clearly and conclusively here. This method only makes sense when it is applied to product comparisons and their properties. You can find a whole lot of information on it on the Internet. Google is very generous when you search for "pairwise comparison". Do not let yourselves be confused by this, this is the standard method used within the field of marketing and the product sector, respectively.

Alright, I have shown you now what you need to be aware of if you set yourself a goal and want to reach it. The list of questions at the beginning, the further explanation of every point as well as the aids and methods, respectively.

I, Christa Nehls, would like to say to you again: You reach goals with stamina, patience, consistency and the use of your very personal pace. I hope you have found new energy to reactivate or newly define your goals. With this in mind, have fun with it.

Exclusiveness
or:
My Truth, Your Truth!

My truth or your truth? That is the question. It sounds like black and white, hot and cold, like polarization and like two extremes. Let us start with an example I heard while waiting in the queue at the optician's:

A woman talked about her daughter having problems. Her psychotherapist talked to the daughter and examined the daughter's childhood, of which the young woman had her own view. The mother rejected exactly this view, spoke of her own truth and added by saying that, after all, she had not read textbooks about it for nothing.

Is it not interesting? We see the things and processes with our own eyes and we deny others to have a view of their own. In our society, it seems to be very difficult to let the others have their own perspective and therefore also their own logic of action.

Is it a case of paternalism if only one's own truth counts? Yes, it is. Is my judgment of this in itself also just about exclusivity, about my own view of things, about my truth? Yes, and yes again. What is all right, socially acceptable and normal is deduced from the general opinion. But, who actually decides what is normal? Our culture, our society, the community. So where does this come from?

Well, a long time before our age, "virtue" was defined. Further information on this can be found on the Internet, for example on Wikipedia or Google Scholar. We know the terms of virtue and vice since antiquity. Within Christian theology, faith as well as hope and love are mentioned by Saint Gregory the Great around the year 600. With regards to secular virtues (Plato, Aristotle, Thomas Aquinas et al.), terms like prudence (knowledge), wisdom and truth or wisdom, justice, courage and temperance can be seen as virtues. Vanity, pride, sloth and lust, on the other hand, count as vices.

"Everyone knows what virtue is in his everyday life. Whether we contemplate our own behavior or make a judgment about the behavior of others, we always let ourselves be guided by specific conceptions of how humans ought to be." Continued: "Virtue is also the good and moral characteristic and basic attitude of a person which is obtained through continuous exercise and self-education and which manifests itself in his or her thoughts and actions as true humanity. Furthermore, virtue is the physical and mental ability obtained by continuous exercise to easily and naturally do that which is perceived as good and valuable in a society."

Let us also look what Bertolt Brecht has to say about this topic in „Verhör des Guten" („Trial of the good man"):

„Step forward:

We have heard that you are a good man. You are not bribable, but the lightning that strikes the house is also not bribable.

What you have once said, you remain true to it. What have you said? You are honest, you say your opinion. Which opinion?

You are brave. In the face of whom? You are wise. For whom?

You don't see to your advantage. To whose do you see? You are a good friend. Also of good people?"

„So hear:

We know you are our enemy. Therefore, we now want to put you up against a wall. But with your achievements and your good characteristics in mind, we want to put you up against a good wall and shoot you with good bullets from good rifles and bury you with a good shovel in good earth."

As long as we make judgments without any knowledge, we are unable to leave people „be", to accept them the way they are. We are not interested in the big picture, we only look at the small fraction we are currently seeing. This is also known as selective perception, or in more scientific terms: tendentious apperception. In colloquial terms, we talk about rose-colored glasses.

Note: Can you still remember physics class? We got to play with pictures and texts in different colors while we were discussing the topic of optics. There were differently colored slides that were laid on top of pictures and texts. Thus, the picture and/or the text changed. Some parts of the picture as well as single words or even whole sentences in the text were missing. Our personal perception works exactly like this, we only see a small part of the whole thing. We only hear and we only feel parts of the whole.

Thus, my truth – your truth is born. The more convinced I am of my truth, the deeper I sink into exclusivity.

Would it not be much more enriching if we were able to see something from multiple perspectives? Would this change of perspectives or paradigms be a benefit for and an expansion of our own consciousness? It implies nothing more than us leaving the accustomed point of view and gaining new impressions and therefore new and different choices by taking a different perspective.

This entails

1. Courage
2. The will to change one's perspective
3. The ability to listen with all senses
4. Letting go

These are four pretty big tasks.

- Courage to dare something new. Deviating from one's accustomed paths and thus abandoning the familiarity of the customary; allowing insecurity and yet daring a new beginning.
- The will to change one's perspective. Courage alone is not enough. Sometimes courage is overwhelmed by so many new and unknown things that courage shrinks again and crawls back into the corner where it came from. Then will comes into play. It supports courage and it helps daring it, it calls to action.
- Listening with all senses: Alfred Adler called it empathy. Seeing with the eyes of the other, hearing with the ears of the other and feeling with the heart of the other. This is a true venture. So much new things await the bold venturer – if it weren't for will, courage would be likely to get smaller again. Based on this listening, it is now important to understand the other. Understanding first is crucial.

- Letting go of the old familiar view, of the accustomed attitude and the usual reaction on the basis of one's own experience (Stephen R. Covey talks about the autobiography here). We really tend to say to one another: "Yes, I am familiar with that, I have also experienced it. Let me tell you what I have done in that situation." Bam – and the connection is gone. Uttering this sentence as the very first one is forbidden. Whether I bring up one of my experiences depends on the given request for help. If someone explicitly asks for it, great, then go for it. But if someone describes a problem or has a question, then listening with all senses is your very first priority. This only works if I let go of everything I want to say before the other person actually starts to communicate.

These four intermediate steps help us letting the others have their truth. They also help us leaving our own truth be for now. Empathizing with someone means putting aside one's own point of view as well as one's own opinion. It also means making room in oneself, accepting and taking the other's point of view into account without abandoning or losing oneself.

With this in mind, I wish you all the best for the discovery of new truths and new shades of grey between black and white and the rest of the color spectrum.

Following New Paths

(Translation: "New paths into a good year.")

Image: Christmas card from 2002 (source unknown)

The other day, I had to chase after one appointment after the other. I had to drive from Heidelberg to Ludwigshafen, to be exact. I had only 45 minutes left, which is normally enough to arrive on time. When I was driving through Mannheim, everything was fine – until I came close to the main station where I got stuck in a traffic jam. Half an hour later, near the Mannheim Palace, I was still laboriously trying to make progress in my car. To be honest, I would have been much faster on foot, but I simply could not leave my car there.

"Very well, you will have to be patient", I said to myself. These words did not really reach my ears somehow, let alone the internal path further inside. I was still impatient. Still trying to overcome my impatience, I saw that the bridge to Ludwigshafen was jammed on three lanes at first, then on two. I made it out of this traffic jam only to get stuck in the next. Worst of all, I eventually found myself on a lane in the exact opposite direction of my destination. My enthusiasm increased in the wrong direction as well. I unconventionally decided to take the empty lane in the middle and found myself at the harbor.

Fortunately, I am from an age where there were no navigation systems yet and my personal sense of direction was still required. That sense of direction got suddenly wide awake on the empty lane. I took the first street to the right out of pure instinct, quickly called the woman of my next appointment at the curbside (I was already running late for my appointed time of arrival) and then followed the few cars. Another instinct had awakened. If also other cars with the same license plate as mine were confidently driving through here, I would simply keep on their tail. Surprisingly, this street immediately lead onto the other bridge to Ludwigshafen, which was almost completely empty, and I arrived at my destination within about 5 minutes, including the time for the phone call. The other route takes almost 10 minutes to drive.

Is it not astonishing how blindly we follow our habits? We have learned, for example, that we feel good if we eat in a specific way. For instance, we only eat cooked food, we do not like raw fruits and vegetables because we get digestive problems if we eat them, because it does not taste good, because…, since … and so on. Only when we are blatantly and clearly confronted with alternative diet options will we maybe change something.

Our attention unmistakably needs to be called to other options from time to time; or we always take the same route to the office although there is a much more comfortable and maybe even shorter route (see above). We have grown used to it.

New paths mean change in our lives. Change means abandoning old (and dear) habits. Abandoning habits means losing a constant in our lives. It means to abandon that which has given us security and confidence so far. Children learn this lesson with their first pacifier, with their first cuddly toy. However, children are still curious and eager to explore. Change is child's play for them, so to speak.

Looking at it in retrospection, I like my "adventure". Without this experience, I would not have had the idea of changing something. I am not sure whether this is going to be my new default route, but I have become more open to change – and I have realized again that diversity is the key.

Well, the city of Ludwigshafen requires drivers to be creative since summer anyway – there are constantly new roadworks in always different places, with known roadworks and new roadway layouts, and with streets that were closed completely in silence and without any understandable reason. Every ride is a new adventure. Every drive is a challenge for fond habits.

Why do the affected people put up with this? Why does it work here? Of course, I can hear storms of rage and complaints about how awful all these roadworks are – those complaints are coming from all sides – but I can also hear a little bit of pioneering spirit. "Have you already tried that route? Between 7 and 8 a.m., it's completely empty." Well, by telling everyone about it, it is not going to be for long… Everybody can contribute good ideas and these ideas are even brought forward with a kind of pride. It is fashionable to be flexible and to discover new things. Naturally, I also want to be complimented for it, else the effort would have been a waste of time, wouldn't it?

Whether you believe it or not: While I was driving along that new route and was realizing where I was, I was thrilled all of a sudden. The route was shorter as well as easier to drive and there was not much traffic. I was amazed that I had not already taken it into consideration much earlier.

That is also the way it is in everyday life. At first, we are upset or even intimidated in the face of impending change. However, as soon as we see and feel the benefits of the new, then enthusiasm slowly and silently begins to grow until it bursts out. And now, at the latest, the time has come to blow one's own horn for this good deed.

Keep going, stay with yourself, use your personal chance, continue. You will keep finding more and more things that are worth changing. You will get even more courageous. You will suddenly realize that life gets easier. Stick to your courage to be open to new things and to try new things. Furthermore, utilize your new found courage to make decisions and to bear the consequences.

Maybe the following sentence can help you here: "Only with empty hands can you reach for the new." This is meant in a figurative sense, of course, and it signifies: Your repertoire of possible actions is used up, your hands are empty. At exactly this point, you and your brain need to be creative, find new solutions, see new paths and follow them.

Do you know Sogyal Rinpoche's autobiography in five chapters from "The Tibetan Book of Living and Dying"? If not, then I will write it down for you:

Chapter 1

I walk along the road.

There is a deep hole in the sidewalk. I fall into it.

I am lost... I am without hope. It is not my responsibility.

It takes forever to get out of it again.

Chapter 2

I walk along the same road.

There is a deep hole in the sidewalk. I pretend not to see it.

I fall into it again.

I cannot believe that I am in the same place again. But it is not my responsibility.

It still takes very long to get out of it.

Chapter 3

I walk along the same road.

There is a deep hole in the sidewalk. I see it.

I still fall into it ... out of habit. My eyes are open.

I know where I am.

It is my own responsibility. I get out of it immediately.

Kapitel 4

I walk along the same road.

There is a deep hole in the sidewalk. I walk around it.

Kapitel 5

I walk along a different road.

April showers...

Spring in the Altes Land, Germany

It is May and lilies of the valley (also known as "may lilies") are flowering outside. Just how do they know that they have to flower now, on time, when the calendar predicts it? Nature looks fresh after the summery day of last week and the rain during the weekend. Everything also looks so new and yet it looks just like every year. Nature sticks to what it knows and especially to what has proven itself.

But aren't we humans doing just the same? We stick with what is known to us and what has proven itself. According to the motto "I prefer known hells to unknown heavens." How is it with us humans? If we do something entirely new, is it really new then or are we just putting an old record into a new record player? Old wine in new bottles? Are we any different to the lilies of the valley in that respect?

We are certainly not on a first glance. On a second glance, however, contemplation silently starts to set in, "if I am like a lily of the valley now, what about me being human?" What does it mean to be a human? Humans have feelings, humans express their feelings (at least often enough), humans make decisions, either consciously or unconsciously. Now the circle closes when we make our decisions unconsciously, that is, when we put an old record into a new record player, we resemble the lily of the valley. We keep our habits and we adapt to them. We always stay on the same track, we just put on different clothes.

If we consciously make decisions, then we face a situation with open eyes, we follow a new path and we leave new tracks. Then we bear the consequences of our own actions even though the path is stony, laborious, unclear, wet, steep and serpentine. We regret our decisions then. Often enough, we do not want to bear the consequences of our decisions and yet exactly this also constitutes a decision in itself. We just wonder a little about this or that thing, about what happens to us. In order to make it a little bit more clear, a couple of specific examples:

Example 1:

Gaining and losing weight...

Sarah and Robert make the decision to stuff their bellies now, fast and easy. The first feeling after it is soothing, their bellies are round and full, it is a warm and cozy feeling. If Sarah and Robert do that over and over again, a whole bunch of pounds will build up. Their weight will increase so much that a simple, regular bathroom scale won't respond anymore. (Nb: If you do not know how much a regular analog scale measures: about 260 to 290 lbs. The modern, digital ones measure up to 330 lbs.) In order to get there, Sarah and Robert have to devour quite a lot of food.

NB: Did you know that around 7,000 kcal equals two pounds of overweight in form of body fat? This certainly is a good investment, also with respect to your finances. The money stays "with you" – as well as every pound.

Let us further suppose that Sarah and Robert have already spent some time successfully losing weight, maybe around 50 / 60 / 100 pounds. They have learned to change their diet and to incorporate exercise into their everyday life. Their health improves day by day, diabetes, high blood pressure, joint pain etc. are almost completely gone and therefore the medications with them. Sarah and Robert become healthier.

...and suddenly, on a nice, bad day, something completely unexpected happens: Robert becomes sick, his back hurts very badly, he is almost unable to move. Sarah has found the apartment of her dreams by chance, moving there and renovating it stresses her out.

Amy, a friend, gets THE chance of further moving up the career ladder and the advanced training takes place alongside her normal job. Now all three of them return to what has always worked well for them, almost their entire life: Sarah, Robert and Amy fall back to their old habits.

Concerning a previously obviously overweight person, this means that he or she eats, eats a lot because this fills the stomach. It is soothing, the belly is round and full, a warm, cozy and almost consoling feeling sets in. Everything around him or her feels warm and comfortable, the stress, the pressure, that being occupied with the old are bearable again. Suddenly – whoosh – the 50 / 60 / 100 pounds are back, and while we are already at it, a few pounds on top of that. What do these laughable 7,000 kcal matter that generate further two pounds of body fat?

I am constantly being asked again and again in my obesity courses: "Why would one do such a thing? Why does this happen to me?" Exactly, why? The participants speculate time and again "I am addicted. I have a food addiction." I cannot and I do not want to say anything to that, it still has not been researched sufficiently. There only is the term of "eating disorders"

Example 2:

New Year's resolutions on New Year's Eve, or something...

Robert has promised to lose lots of pounds; Mary finally wants to do her boaters license; Tom intends to quit smoking in the new year; Lily finally wants to do more for herself, read books, work out, do relaxation exercises and eat healthy. All of this works out pretty well at first.

Robert has joined a weight loss group because he does not want to be alone. Mary has got out her books again in order to read half an hour every day. Tom has read up on the subject in books and has talked to an alternative practitioner who gives him an acupuncture treatment. He does not have the courage to do it himself. Lily was at the gym and has registered for various courses in order to get fit and learn relaxation techniques. In order to be on the safe side, she has already registered for six months and has paid the fees in advance.

But just as it always is in life, everyday life catches up on every one of them. Tom smokes more than ever before, the acupuncture needles drove him crazy, he now craves his cigarettes even more.

But everything was so neatly planned out, the books, the needles – the craving for cigarettes would surely vanish all by itself. However, he forgot to make himself responsible as well.

Lily's twin sister becomes sick. She cannot think clearly anymore, she is afraid she might have the same disease in her, she worries about her sister and her life, she forgets herself – and the gym.

Mary has been consistently working with her books for several weeks now. She has made a studying plan and she studies daily, if possible. She sets herself goals for what chapters she wants to have learned from one week to the next. She consistently keeps going, occasionally skips a day of learning in order to relax and do something different. The next day she is going to register for the theoretical exam. If she passes, she can register for the practical exam.

Robert becomes sick, it is his back. He eats passionately again. Three weeks later, however, he calls it quits. He gets help and talks about what has happened. He vaguely remembered a sentence he learned during the program: "There is no shame in falling down. True shame is to not stand up again." Although he was caught in a depressed mood for a short time

("Nothing matters anymore") and regretted his relapse, this sentence still caught up on him.

Conclusion

Unwanted, surprising events interrupt newly gained processes and new habits. These new processes, actions, rituals and habits are not stable yet. Quite to the contrary, they are still very delicate and fragile, just like a young flower in the garden. Thus, (almost) everything is forgotten again, the old habits are stronger, almost as if they were cast in stone. The new flowers wither because they are not "watered" anymore.

My experience shows that it is always the habits. Everybody has habits that, depending on the age, had more or less time to leave their marks in the brain.

A small digression: By the way, do you know the old hollow ways that were used in the past for the transportation of practically everything on a wagon? The "Hohle Gasse" ("hollow alleyway") near Küssnacht, Switzerland, through which William Tell allegedly went, consists of stone that is covered with moss and that was shaped by wagon tracks. In the past, the area surrounding it was made up of swampland that stretched between the lakes. This hollow way was the only way across the mountains between Lake Zug and Lake Lucerne.

During the course of many centuries, wagon tracks have dug deeper and deeper into the stone – so deep that only wagons are still able to move there; other vehicles would get stuck. Habits work quite similarly in our brain, they dig extremely deep tracks or marks. They are so strong in us that we have to give it our all in order to wean ourselves off these habits again.

The fond and dear habits can only be let go by Sarah, Amy, Lily and Tom as soon as they do not love these habits anymore. Robert and Mary have found a way. While Robert still has to ward off a last hint of insecurity, Mary has gained utter security. Her goal is in her direct reach. Both of them have made the clear decision to take responsibility for themselves.

As nice as it is to be told something, to read an instructional book, to undergo treatment (e.g. acupuncture needles in one ear, stomach- reduction surgery etc.), it does not really change anything, the respective person remains rigid. Only when he or she does something, i.e. actively starts acting or doing something, will change come. At first cautiously, practicing, feeling, but actively doing something. The more you practice, the more security you will gain, the stronger and more robust the delicate flower called "new habit" will become, the stronger you become and the more stable the new habit becomes.

Have you noticed it? Actions speak louder than words, actively doing something matters. You will need courage for this and you will need even more courage for keeping it up, changing something and incorporating new things into your life. The general maxim is now called: PRACTISE, PRACTISE, PRACTISE. And when you are done with that: PRACTISE, PRACTISE, PRACTISE. With all my heart I wish you all the best, good luck, lots of courage, strength and even more persistence in your changes. Take the responsibility for yourself, bear the consequences. You will not regret it – after all, it is for the most precious possession of yours, it is for yourself.

Lastly, do not forget: "There is no shame in falling down. True shame is to not stand up again."

Actually…

"Now that I think about it, I should…"

ACTUALLY...

... I already wanted to write about the topic of saying goodbye a year ago.

...I already wanted to publish a new newsletter months ago.

... I have wanted to read a particular book for quite some time now.

... I wanted to call / visit someone specific.

... I wanted to take greater care of myself again.

Are you also familiar with this? Actually... our good intentions that we postpone again and again, that we do not put into practice because of various reasons. I almost wrote "these issues that we do not tackle" right now. That is exactly the reason why we have so much problems putting these plans into practice. For us, it seems necessary to make an extra effort, it seems almost necessary to fight for it. Otherwise we would be afraid of not getting it done. Fighting, however, impedes rather than helps us.

Actually,... I wanted to write something about the topics of saying goodbye, dying and death together with a terminally ill friend of mine one year ago. During spring of 2009, he said, o, no, not now. Everybody writes about that during spring, fall and winter. Let's write about it in August." But this was not to be. His condition worsened in August, the treatment was terminated as it did not have any effect and he died in a hospice in September. Over and over again, he said "Everything is done and ready in my head. Now I only need a computer and then we can start writing." But death came quicker.

Actually, I then wanted to write and publish the text on my own just in order to realize that I was unable to do so as long as my mourning was left unattended and unfinished in the corner; until… and in the first place… and actually…

Yes, I have finished mourning. A different newsletter will deal with the topic of saying goodbye and death. Only this time, dear reader, it is just going to be contemplative and even a little bit philosophical, so do not be surprised.

Actually… is the sister of "If I had just…". What exactly could we have actually done if we had just done it? The famous German poet Johann Wolfgang von Goethe had – once again – something appropriate to say regarding this subject: "Knowing is not enough; we must apply. Willing is not enough; we must do."

We have also reached a crucial point here: The things we always wanted to do, but which are never done, are eventually forgotten. Then regret, remorse and desperation sets in: "If I had just…" As you now understand, I haven't mentioned the creeping death of my friend without a reason. We actually always wanted to do, but we never did. That is a shame because there was no second chance for us to write about saying goodbye and death together.

What about those missed chances? We usually regret them. How would it be if we asked instead what we otherwise do with our time? Is there something that seems more important to me? Is there something that fascinates me so deeply that I neither think about nor do anything else anymore? In this case, mentioning the seemingly missed chance really made sense. Something much more important, maybe even something much more personal is waiting to be done by you. There is no "actually ...", there is just saying "yes" to action.

Immediately stop your complaints about missed chances, there are innumerable new chances and opportunities. Your complaints just prevent you from seeing and taking them. So whatever it is, a new dress, a book, a car, a walk, a vacation, a talk with a dear person, do it. RIGHT NOW! As long as you do it, there are no missed chances about which you need to complain. By the way, Alfred Adler once said regarding this topic: "The biggest danger in life is to be too cautious."

You have always wanted to try out something entirely new? Do it before it turns into a missed chance. An example from/ about me:

In spring, I have decided that I want to learn how to play snooker, a highly strategic version of billiards. For more than 20 years, I have watched the players in TV broadcasts and listened to the commentary of Rolf Kalb, a German sports commentator. I have now taken some lessons and I practice at the billiards table.

In August, I even attended a big snooker tournament in Southern Germany. I hesitated beforehand: "Do I really need to do this, does this make sense? Don't I have something better and more important to do?" The answer was "maybe", but the experience called "tournament" was even more important to me. I have also met other people who are interested in this sport and who also call themselves fanatics. We talked and we all agreed that this sport can make you humble, sometimes even angry. Angry when the billiard balls just do not want sink into the pockets. These billiard balls are actually quite annoying. Un-actually, however, the balls are simply doing exactly what the player does to them since they do not have a will of their own. There will be more on this topic in another newsletter.

In summary: I have done it and I got out of the "Actually, I would like to play snooker." Now only practicing remains to be done.

With this in mind: Please leave the "actually…" and "If I had just…" behind. Become the designer of your life and decide consciously what you do and what not. Then there are no missed chances anymore.

As always, the only thing left for me to say is: "Keep practicing, practice makes perfect." Well, and while you are practicing, do not forget: "There is no shame in falling down. True shame is to not stand up again." So keep practicing consistently and hang on.

Stay true to yourself and your wishes.

Snooker or the New Form of Humility?

Snooker table ready for play
Snookerhall Mannheim, Germany

You might still remember that I told you about how I overcame my personal "Actually...". I learned to play snooker. Of course you ask justly what snooker has to do with humility and what it is doing here.

Well, life is quite complicated sometimes. Nothing works out the way it should. Everything was thought through and planned so nicely. Then, suddenly, nothing works the way it was meant to work. That is just the way it is in snooker.

Let us start with the explanation of snooker. Wikipedia states, among other things, that "Snooker is a version of the precision sport of billiards that is played with special cues on a snooker table. The goal of the game is to shoot fifteen red and six differently colored object balls ("color balls") into the pockets according to specific rules by striking the white cue ball." and "In comparison with other popular forms of cue sports, snooker has a higher technical difficulty and requires its players to have more sophisticated tactical abilities. The higher technical difficulty, compared with many other versions of billiard sports, is mainly due to the greater playing surface of the table and the smaller diameter of the balls. Furthermore, the pockets are cut further into the rails and are narrower...".

Because of this description, you certainly understand that many things in snooker are also nicely thought through and planned (planning shots in advance like the moves in chess) while, in the end, the ball does not even remotely think of falling into the pocket; not to mention that the ball moves into exactly that position the player wants it to be or needs it to be in order to take the follow-up shot. To be honest, this makes the player desperate or causes him to have a fit of rage sometimes. However, this is absolutely not going to persuade the ball to reconsider, even if it is the goal of the game to shoot all object balls off the table one by one with adequately skillful shots and well-placed balls.

Flashback: Since approximately 1990, maybe even earlier than that, I have been watching TV broadcasts of snooker tournaments, I know most of the top 100 players by name or even by sight. Sometimes I even know their playing style as well. In 2007 and 2010, I attended two exhibition matches between Ken Doherty and Joe Swail (both of whom are players of the World Tour, similar to the ATP World Tour in tennis etc.), and then, in August, I attended a real snooker tournament for the very first time: the ranking tournament in Fürth.

Enough of the preliminary reports and explanations, let us turn to the main thing now: From May until June, I took lessons from a private coach and started having first reasonably good results. "The rest is only a matter of practice", the coach said. This certainly reminds you of many previous issues of this newsletter: PRACTICE, PRACTICE, PRACTICE. You know this if you acquire a profession, if you learn to play an instrument, if you go ice skating or if you learn to ride a bike or drive a car. Learning means practicing, it means to internalize processes until you know them by heart. Thus, I stand at the table again and again at random intervals and think about how to pocket the balls; I "actually" dream of standing at the table several times a week and thus speeding up my learning curve. I dream of playing proper games on the table. But first, I need to attend to my technique, the different aspects of the shot, effect and direction of the shot in relation to the ball and so much more.

As a counselor, a consultant and as a coach, I am constantly required to have creative solutions and ideas for actions up my sleeve. In addition, there is also a demand for cheerful words and phrases for the one seeking counsel / the client / the one being coached to continue or even dare do something at all.

Interestingly, my snooker coach unknowingly illustrated exactly these coaching situations to me. I have also incorporated the phrases he used for cheering me up into my own repertoire later. I was amazed, what was this all about? Should a snooker coach actually have the same kind of skills a business coach has? Apparently, yes – if I examine the following event. What do you think?

One day in the snooker hall: I missed every single shot. I was unable to pocket a single ball. Suddenly, my coach said that I should put the cue on the table and leave the table. I was a little surprised, but I did as I was told. He asked me to wait a moment, then he vanished and returned from the bar shortly after with a glass of water. He handed it to me and asked me to drink it. Once again, I did as I was told and let the cool water run down my throat. Then he took the glass again and put it away. He said that I should concentrate, do my preparations, go back to the table and simply make the shot. This time, the ball immediately disappeared in the pocket.

What had happened? On the one hand, my attention was brought to another objective, in this case: getting away from the table and drinking. It resulted in a clear interruption of my previous action, namely, the unsuccessful pocketing of the balls, the experience of failure, the feeling of being unable to do it, the stopping of the mistakes. Let go! Body and spirit could relax. Concentrating on the ball that should be pocketed was possible after that. Aiming, shooting, pocketing. I had done it!

Let us return to tennis again. When Boris Becker started to misplay his tennis balls during a game, he always changed his shirt or his racquet. So he would do nothing else in such a situation, he brought his attention to something else, concentrated again and – voilà – everything went smoothly again.

An essential experience to make while learning was to keep going, not to give up and to keep hanging on.

I could strengthen the following characteristics in me by playing, which turned it (almost) into child's play:

- Perseverance
- Stamina
- Consistency
- Patience
- Concentration

Now humility comes into play again. Not everything works on the first try, practice makes perfect, success is a part of every failure, these are the mottos of the day. We need a little bit of humility again. So many things are beyond our control and we are not masters of every situation. Humility helps and encourages us to keep going. Humility means peace and it therefore supports us in getting a new perspective on the world around us. Humility enables us to achieve something through our own effort and determination. So let's better meet every learning experience with the appropriate amount of humility and attention. Anger and wrath are of no use, they let us lose our sense of proportion and thus obstruct our view on the essential things. The joy of achievement as well as consistency and perseverance consolidate the things that we have learned.

The Irish snooker coach P.J. Nolan says in one of his books (freely memorized):

There are eight basic goals in learning the game:

1. Analyzing do you have the right posture? Positive mental attitude?
2. Learning through observation (of other players)
3. Evaluation of one's own game, of one's mistakes.
4. People player, coach, manager are all equally important for professionals
5. Practicing developing a routine
6. Patience with oneself at the table and also beyond the table
7. Time management don't waste time, but keep "actually" in mind
8. Having fun, enjoying, recognizing one's own progress even if one plays or practices alone

Surprisingly, these basic rules apply to every area where you want to achieve something, such as driving a car or playing the piano, and so on.

Current events: The topicality of events catches up with me once again. Snooker has become a little tedious during the last couple of years – at least watching it has. 35 frames are a long time for both spectators and players. Since 2010, an entirely new wind is blowing through the snooker halls and tournaments. There are new tournament modes like PTC and EPTC. There are tournaments that (are supposed to) fill the "silly season" a bit and, since very recently, there is power snooker. Suddenly, all the supposedly so serious players are quick again and full of enthusiasm, the audience is carried away and not so shy and reserved anymore, cheers sound through the hall and when it should become too quiet, Shaun Murphy ignites the audience anew. The games only last a couple of frames now, about 5 to 7 of them. A new age of snooker dawns, the old is being let go.

You see, everything repeats and everything is new. It remains exciting. Not long ago, I read in a forum: "Creativity is the art of making the known look new."

Another word about learning. Soon, I am going to write something about the subject of learning. Together with others, I am going to think about the things that are old and have grown dear to us and I am going to contemplate what new there is to say on this subject and what we all find useful in which context. I will also certainly refer to one or another thing I have already written here.

Say so long, but not goodbye...

Starlings ready for departure

"One can recognize a true goodbye by it not hurting anymore".
Hans Noll (*1954), German author and graphic designer

During the summer of 2008, Peter and I decided to write a newsletter about saying goodbye and dying. This intention is everything that remained. Peter died in a hospice in September 2009.

This was a completely new experience for me, staying by a friend's side until the very end and repeatedly talking to him about it.

So we once asked ourselves who gets to decide whether someone leaves this world. We agreed that the one who wants to go gets to decide when it is time. If he has still something or much to do, then this time will be postponed. Death also has its due time, just like everything else has its due time.

Many different thoughts went through his mind, such as the worry about his family, for whom he always felt responsible, the worry about friends or the worry about acquaintances who need his help. However, he always forgot the worry about himself. I tirelessly pointed it out to him. Until he said one day: "My angel, you are so right and I always think that others are more important. I still have so many things to do." But time was already running short then. It was May 2009.

During this time, a friend told me that there is a popular saying: "Angels accompany a soul into the other world." She added by saying: "You are someone's angel, and then it is your task to make sure that the soul finds its way home and is guided there." I thought that this was a huge responsibility. Nevertheless, I could carry it reasonably easily.

Marcus, a long-term friend of Peter, and I met in front of Peter's door in the hospital during the last weeks. Since then, we were taking care of one another and were also taking care of Peter together. In the hospice, the staff was taking care of us and made sure that we were rationing our strength.

A verse from a song of Trude Herr crosses my mind again and again: "One never leaves completely, something of me remains here." From this time with Peter, I have learned how important it is to live in the present moment, in the here and now. I have learned how important it is to take good care of yourself and to go the last section of your way consciously. Maybe even how important it is to decide what my last days are going to look like (e.g. living will, health care proxy, funeral, last resting place, organ donor registry).

A part of him is still here. His delight in enjoyment, his delight in good talks, his caring, his laughter. But also his grumpiness if he did not like something or if something was contrary to his view of the world (again), when he could not understand the actions of other people or even thought of them as bad or awful. A part of him is still here.

I have also learned during this time how important it is to face this last goodbye with all your consciousness. Not only this very last path, death, but also every other path that leads to a goodbye.

Similarly, the separation from

- people (e.g. Marriage / relationship),
- a job or a profession,
- a place of residence or a neighbor,
- home and garden,
- something of one's own, something self-made, e.g. house, company, foundation etc.,
- a piece of one's body through a surgery
- physical independence, e.g. walking on crutches or sitting in a wheelchair

Saying goodbye takes consciousness. Saying goodbye takes contemplation, the thinking about what happened. It requires the appreciation of all events that have been experienced together.

A couple of days ago, I listened to the audiobook "Cancer – Schmancer" by Fran Drescher ("The Nanny"). In this book, she talks about her struggle due to doctors not taking her symptoms seriously until she undergoes surgery just in time before severe methods of treatment like radiation therapy, chemotherapy etc. had to be begun.

Among other things, she says that there was only about one week left between the diagnosis and the actual surgery and that she therefore had no time to deal with this topic. In particular, she had no time to understand what the removal of the female reproductive organs would mean for her and her future life. All of this came only after the surgery and it manifested itself in the form of tiredness, listlessness, exhaustion, lack of vitality, tears, regrets and missed chances.

I hear similar things from clients with regards to separations or divorces. As long as everything goes its way, the only thing that is being done is to function. Only afterwards does the process of understanding and emotional digestion set in.

Many things would be easier if we approached the topic consciously. Only few events occur suddenly, from one moment to the next. Most events foreshadow themselves so that we can approach them consciously. We can think about what would be, if... ; we can strain our imagination to picture possible outcomes and then find a way of achieving these outcomes.

Mourning is a taboo in our society (see also Pütz-Roth: "Trauer braucht eine Heimat" ("Mourning needs a home")). If a person mourns another person, he or she is supposed to be done with it and return to his everyday routine after only a short time. Many feel embarrassed to see people mourn or cry even. Just return to the norm as quickly as possible. But what is the norm?

We have lost every sense of normality. This is normal: death is an integral part of life. We have already "bought" it alongside our birth. So there are no choices like the ones you are used to when buying a new car: "Please no headlight washing system or something like that. No."

Death is an integral part of life. Saying goodbye is an integral part of life. Change is an integral part of life.

Yes, I can hear the voices saying again: "Change, how terrible! How confusing! How awful!" And from far back, from the last rows, I hear very few voices shouting: "Change, how exciting! Something gets going."

This is how diverse people are. It is so important to allow for change to happen in life, to see what beautiful and good things can emerge from it instead of reacting fearfully and wanting to leave everything the way it was.

Life means change, it is like a train into which we get on the day of our birth. More people get in on the way, get into the train compartment or just into a different car. Other people get out. We, on the other hand, stay on the train and continue traveling through our lives until we reach the end of the line. Thus, every goodbye causes a change since something leaves our lives. And if I may cite Trude Herr once again: "One never leaves oneself completely, something of you comes along, it will always have its place with me." We always carry with us a part of what we have seen, experienced, learned, tasted, smelled and felt.

In family companies that – for whatever reason – are to be sold or even shut down shortly, there is very much mourning present and great difficulties have to be let go there. So much own strength, money and lifetime and so many own thoughts, ideas and memories have been put into this. Saying goodbye to this hurts.

Saying goodbye to the partner hurts, many good as well as bad times have been shared. It is all part of the big picture.

A woman slowly became a pain patient. She could hardly walk anymore, she had to sit in a wheelchair eventually. She mourned her old life. Then she decided to arrange various memories on a wall. During the course of time, she dealt with every single one of them, remembered, let go and said goodbye to them. She also did similar things with a pair of high heels, for example. She had kept them for a long time, but after a certain amount of time the moment had come to say goodbye to these dear shoes as well and therefore to say goodbye to a chapter of her life too. In this way, she made room for her present life in order to let new things enter it, to be able to recognize the new and to accept the new.

Saying goodbye means something different for everybody and yet the same for all. Saying goodbye is a part of life and ensures growth. Just like the fruit that falls down from the tree and becomes earth. The seeds are in the soil and will be the source for new life.

I will say goodbye to you here while knowing that I will meet you again in this exact place. Furthermore, I hope that you have gained good and useful insights for your everyday life.

> „...One never leaves completely,
> something of me remains here,
> it will always have its place with you.
>
> One never leaves oneself completely,
> something of you comes along,
> it will always have its place with me."
>
> *Trude Herr*

Lifelong Learning

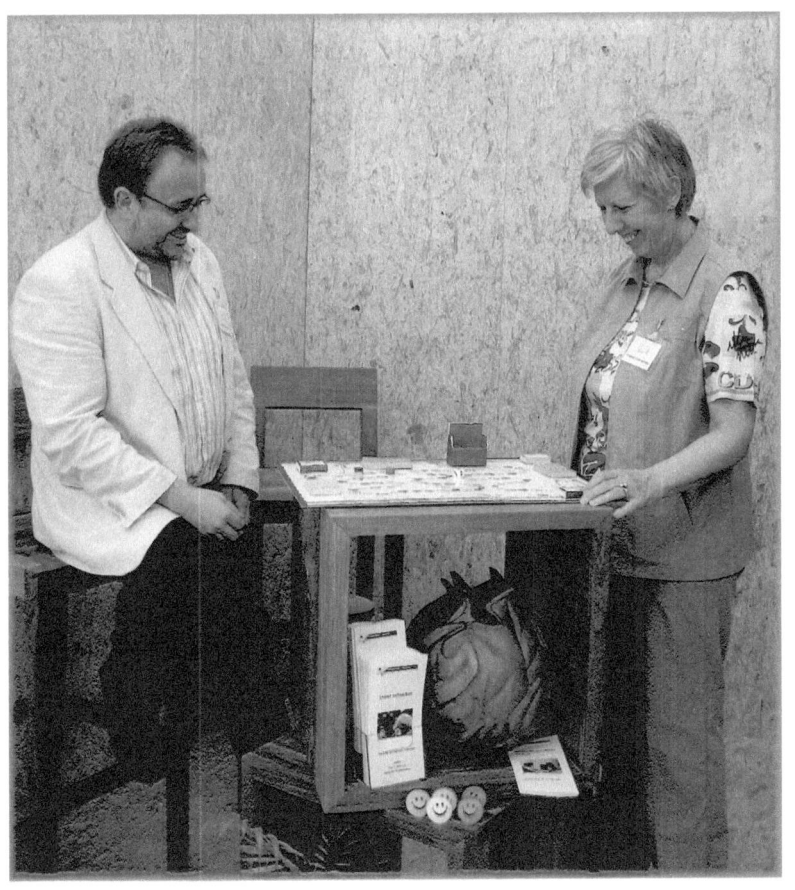

Ingrid C. and Harald H.
Learn through play „Mon Tresor"

"Non scholae sed vitae discimus"

This means: We do not learn for the school, but for life.

Some time ago, I noticed the following phrase in my calendar: "You are on earth in order to learn."

It almost sounds like a threat, always learning, never resting, keeping going and going, no rest. But that is certainly not meant by that. It rather is an invitation, that is, every moment in life can be a moment for learning and understanding.

As a coach and consultant, I have to master the challenge of appropriately preparing content for and presenting it to individuals or entire groups of people on a daily basis. This does not only mean to convey knowledge, but also to learn for yourself. The only things I can convey to people successfully and well are the things I understood myself; not to mention conveying these things in such a way so that they can be put into practice in everyday life. All according to my motto: "ACTIONS speak louder than words."

A long time ago, Confucius said:

"Tell me, and I will forget it.
Show me, and I will remember it.
Let me do it, and I will understand it."

Many studies from the 1990s and earlier supported this statement. Stefan Aufenanger[3] comments on a study done by the University of Siegen (Germany) in June 2000. It looked at the amount of information gathered and memorized during human learning processes and expressed it in percent of the original information input. Stefan Aufenanger comments as follows: "The often cited idea, mostly even expressed graphically, that humans can only memorize 10 percent of what they read, 20 percent of what they heard, 30 percent of what they saw, 50 percent of what they heard and saw, and 90 percent of what they did is a naïve assumption and this simplistic cumulation is not supported by any serious scientific experiment. The reason for this is that many factors come into play during learning with new media so that a reduction to such a simplistic learning theory does not even come close to the actual reality of learning."*

More recent approaches distinguish between four different learning types to which the older learning theory described above is not applicable anymore. These new learning types include:

1. visual
2. auditory
3. kinesthetic
4. auditory-digital

---

[3]http://www.tu-dresden.de/sulifg/dag/fumedien/multimedia.html (German)

The joy of learning, curiosity about the subject, positive emotions, over-extension / under-challenge and exercise are also significant factors.

Randy Pausch (University professor, deceased in 2008) was convinced that we can only learn really successfully by having fun. However, he also said that it also requires honest, solid and serious feedback which conveys to the learner that somebody is interested in him or her, even if that person is not smiling at that moment. It also conveys that that particular person trusts the learner to be able to do it.

1.1 For what purpose do we learn?

There is an almost infinite number of answers to that question, such as on principle, in order to further develop, making progress or making a career, being able to move better, improving one's health, standing out amongst other people, keeping your brain fit, satisfying one's own curiosity…

Learning for the sake of learning. But only with joy, fun, ease, feedback and encouragement from oneself or others. Most people learn to develop socially as well as professionally, be independent and keep their finger on the pulse of the times.

In fact, research suggests: there is no success without learning. Furthermore, the more curious we are, the better we understand and keep the information. Curiosity always means having a great interest in something.

1.2 State of my research

The subject of learning made me curious and thus I searched in all kinds of media for what news there is about it. In summary, I can say on the one hand that the discovery of learning types is prevailing and on the other that methods like super learning, power reading etc. are up-and-coming. Moreover, the psyche should certainly be taken into account as well. I also had an essential realization that learning is perceived as a very individual process nowadays and that no generalization whatsoever is applied to it, in contrast to what many old sayings could make you believe.

In relevant literature, fun can be repeatedly found in the context of learning. This has nothing to do with a hedonistic attitude in our society, but it rather expresses the simple joy of discovering new things or exploring unknown territories. Thus, it can be easily inferred that learning in the presence of fear or pressure will not achieve good results. However, we can only be successful if we learn.

Recently a good acquaintance of mine said to me: "I have made it my goal to learn something new every year. It has to be something that has neither something to do with my job nor my previous interests or hobbies. Thus, I stay vigorous, curious and interested." He left me thoughtful. Then I realized: "I have already done this my entire life, I just haven't thought about it yet."

Right now, you are probably wondering what one could do if he or she were to do such a thing. Here are a few suggestions from my own experience:

- drawing comics
- developing your voice with the help of an opera singer
- playing the piano
- playing snooker
- Qigong
- writing for a newspaper

But it is your job to be creative here. What else can you think of? What have you always wanted to try out? It is not the purpose to become a master in this activity, being a mere student can also be quite satisfying.

Let us take a closer look at the different learning types:

- visual type, senses via sight and can visualize inner images well
- auditory type, senses via hearing; when he visualizes something, then he rather hears other people's comments that he heard when he reached the visualized object.

- kinesthetic type, senses via touch and movement; when he visualizes something, he rather perceives the feeling he had when he reached the object.
- auditory-digital type, a strictly logical person. When he visualizes something, he does not see anything most of the time and has he difficulty to relax.

There is hardly anyone who can be matched to just one of these four learning types. Most people are mixed types with a personal focus on one of the types described above.

Further information (in German):
http://www.topos-online.at/html-texte/wahrtyp.htm

You would like to know what learning type you are? Here is a link (German): www.hpz.com/sinneskanal.pdf. According to Hans-Peter Zimmermann, this test is 80% accurate.

1.2.1 Exercise

You are asking yourself right now what exercise has to do with learning? This is an interesting piece of information for me as well. Exercise is responsible for the formation of more neurons. This means: you like to go for a walk and you put on the headphones of your player and everything that you hear while walking will stick in your memory better. Is that not a fascinating thought, killing two birds with one stone?

1.2.2 Attention, Concentration and Focussing

Do not spread your attention. There is, of course, the saying that women are capable of multitasking, which means that women are allegedly capable of doing multiple things simultaneously. This myth was disproven in several recent studies, so men can breathe a sigh of relief. But what does multitasking have to do with learning success? The greater your focus on one thing is, the greater the resulting effect will be.

A simple example: You are on the phone with someone and you are responding to an e-mail at the same time. Both recipients will notice that you weren't paying full attention to them while answering. Our brain notices that too. You are eating and reading the newspaper or watching TV, well, the stomach will not notice that it is getting food. The result is that you will not get satiated. Moreover, it is exactly the same with learning: if you learn something only with a part of your attention, you will miss a great deal of information. So only learn with your full attention and concentration.

1.2.3 Keeping the Balance

Be careful not to undergo negative stress. You need a balance between the requirements and your own capabilities. In order to achieve this, you need positive stress, that is, taking joy in satisfying the requirements. Positive stress leaves "marks" in the brain, so called memory marks. You have done something with great joy and have met the requirements at the same time, even under time pressure. This experience remains in the memory mark and it even digs further in.

I know that experience from playing snooker. I can ponder on a single ball for quite some time in order to practice in what angle I have to shoot the cue ball on the object ball for it to sink in a pocket. My brain remembers that. But if I do not get the right technique for a longer period of time, I will slowly but surely become frustrated.

Now negative stress starts to set in. My neurons lack energy, they are undersupplied. Because of this, the region of my brain that is responsible for memory and learning is disturbed, under permanent stress it is even damaged. This brain region is called the hippocampus, and it is so sensitive that it could almost be described as a sissy. Relaxation breaks are important in order to bring back motivation.

1.2.4 Emotions

Does this sound familiar? You are occupied with something and it is fun. You go with the flow, you practically swim along, you are in utter harmony with yourself, the world and the requirement you currently have to meet. Spitzer describes this state as "inner participation". Thus, learning successes are activated, the reward system (dopamine system) awakens and kick-starts our learning turbo. Mihály Csíkszentmihályi uses the term "flow".

1.2.5 Motivation

Probably everybody will say now: "My motivation, that's the most important thing." Not only from what you have already read in the text. "To be motivated," I ask myself, "does it make sense what I'm doing right now?" If I look at the example of my beloved snooker, I say yes because I want to get better, want to pot multiple balls one after the other, want to stay at the table. It helps me to improve my stamina, my concentration, my perseverance and my patience (see "Snooker or the New Form of Humility"). As I see and appreciate my own successes again and again, I stay motivated.

In summary, it can be stated that endogenous opiates are released by the dopamine system through the combination of keeping balance, emotions and self-motivation. The reward system works at its maximum, and within us the enthusiastic realization arises: "another obstacle defeated."

Consolidating and keeping this learning success requires only one action: "Practice, practice, practice!" Now you know why I always keep playing the same ball so often and for such a long time. The repetition consolidates my knowledge in my brain and in my subconscious so that it can be accessed later without me even thinking about it.

Let me summarize again what this means for one's everyday life:

- Consciously use all your senses. Hear the birds singing and recognize which birds they are. Listen to the wind between the leaves. Look at the clouds, observe how they change, how they never stay the same. Touch and feel. Be creative while you do this.

- Do unfamiliar things: write something at your desk while you are standing, swap your knife and fork while eating, start using the mouse with your left hand instead of your right hand, or the other way around. Put your recycle bin in a different place. Once again, your creativity is requested.

- Stay curious. Keep discovering new things within your own home, outside while doing a walk, while talking to neighbors. Stay awake and alert. If something has caught your special interest, gather information about it from books or the Internet or from other people who know something about it.

- Consciously exercise your memory. Say in advance what the name of the next freeway exit is when you drive to work. Learn your shopping list by heart and leave it at home on purpose

- Drive on / follow new paths; see chapter "Following New Paths"

You might say now that you were done with learning for now. I can truly understand that. While I was doing the research for this chapter, I had some major "misfirings" from time to time; I did not want to learn anymore. Even if I had wanted to, it was a dead end. I did not have fun and the information was presented in a way I absolutely did not like. Talking about learning types: I have to see and hear it, sometimes also feel it, to memorize it properly. Pictures are good for my memorizing ability. If I had none of that, I would not make any progress in my research.

1.3 The Interviews

I have already planned this newsletter for a long time and I have even asked some people around me to fill out a questionnaire on the subject of learning. The following questions were important to me:

- Why do we learn?
- Which personal motivation for learning do you have?
- When do you learn best?
- How do you learn best?
- How and when do you learn easiest?
- When is it absolutely no fun to learn?
- Have you already experienced the Eureka effect while learning? What effect does it have in your case?
- Lust for learning or learning enthusiasm – do such things exist?

- Teachers and coaches talk about learning types. Are you familiar with these learning types? What type are you?
- Our information society condemns us to learn during our entire lives. What reaction does this statement trigger in you?

I have received various responses which were as diverse as the people who have given them.

NB: If you are in the mood for it, why not answer the questions yourself? You can send me your results if you like. The responses are going to be used by me as anonymous statements, but not in any personalized form whatsoever.

An evaluation of the interviews will follow.

Health and Exclusiveness – Plea for a holistic medicine

This time it is going to be a short newsletter in between. The evaluation of the interviews on the subject of learning are promised and not forgotten. Forbearance is no acquittance, I can assure you.

Lately another subject has crossed my mind more often and more vigorously than ever before. It is the subject of health and therapy caught between Eastern and Western culture, between classical and alternative, between nature and the pharmaceutical industry, between miracle healing and not being responsive to any treatment anymore, between trust and ignorance.

Caution, I am just thinking out loud this time and I want to blow off some steam. I want to rant and wonder about the exclusiveness with which we evaluate something, with which we deem something "good" or condemn it. The mentioned pairs of words – sometimes contrasts, sometimes only in the same context – indicate seeming contradictions between the particular topics.

During the 1990s, the German news magazine "Der Spiegel" had a whole series of specials on the future of humanity. The new age was defined: the information society. The Internet makes us smarter and smarter – and maybe also more and more stupid.

In one of these specials, Eastern medicine – or rather Chinese medicine, to be exact – as well as Western medicine were discussed. I can still remember a specific part of it: A Chinese physician said that he has come to the West just to study medicine there, bring this knowledge back home afterwards and to combine it with Chinese medicine. He said he intended to incorporate new things, get rid of outdated customs and synthesize the benefits of both Eastern and Western medicine.

He also said that he could not understand the people in the West throwing away their own knowledge and skills to substitute it with TCM (traditional Chinese medicine), for example. Furthermore, he stated that a great number of things in TCM were incomprehensible to people from the West. Chinese children are fed it with their mother's milk, so to speak. This includes specific behavior, the attitude towards life, environment, society and a mentality that can only emerge from this culture. TCM originated in this environment. According to him, it was the same way around with Western medicine.

What is wrong with us in the West that we are unable to appreciate what we have? Why do we always have to chase after all the new and trendy things just because someone suggests that his or her teachings are the only true and correct ones? What motivates us? How many things do we need to hype up, until we wake up and form our own opinion? When will we finally learn to listen to our body, get reliable information and then to act according to our own needs instead of running after the next trend?

Properly finding and evaluating information needs to be learned as well. Most things one can find on the Internet will not stand any test whatsoever, especially not the test of common sense. So what needs to be done?

Well, the only thing that helps is learning and understanding. Using common sense, thinking about the things that have been found: How does this fit into this existing reality? What is good for me? Do I really need to swallow another active substance or does exercise, having a good talk or simply a day spent relaxing also do the trick of giving my body air to breathe and to live?

We have lost our sense of self, we mostly see ourselves as a bunch of symptoms and every single symptom should be cured individually. Moreover, we have forgotten that we are one whole thing, we have forgotten that it is of no use to get a diagnosis and to treat the corresponding illness. If we have a cold, it is a great relief to have a nose spray for free airways, aspirin for headaches, and something that alleviates the cough. However, the body needs more than pure medications: he longs for rest and the immune system cries for support in fighting off the germs. Neither nose spray nor painkillers or cough syrup can offer that. The only thing that can really help here are a couple of days rest in bed, drinking enough water to support blood circulation or get it going, and light food. This is a holistic approach, being one with yourself and with nature. Our grandparents' generation still knew that, we since seem to have lost it somewhere along the way.

I plead for thinking first and seeing what is good for me before taking action. Face your therapist as a mature and well-informed person. Ask questions if you do not understand something. If you have doubts, ask for time for consideration before accepting a (proposed) treatment. If something does not go according to plan during the treatment, ask about it. This is what your physician is for, he or she accompanies you during the treatment. It is also his job to take your questions and worries seriously.

You object justly by asking: "What about an accident, especially a life-threatening one?" Just do as the Chinese do: Trust the capabilities of the therapists that are from the same cultural area where you grew up.

Hippocrates already said: "Not the physician, but nature cures. The physician can only be its loyal helper and servant. The physician will learn from nature, but nature will never learn from the physician."

And this applies to all forms of cures and methods of treatment. All of them are only as good as the relationship between the one who treats and the one who is treated. This relationship is based on trust – without trust, there is no successful treatment. If you decide not to accept certain medications or therapies, cures, etc. that were ordered otherwise, talk about it with the physician who ordered it.

People around me often tell me that they treat themselves, that they buy their own medications and that they know what is best for them. In such situations, I often wonder: "What the hell was their major at college…?!"

At least there already seems to be a certain degree of change going on in our medical society: An individualization of treatment is occurring, separated from the mass industry. Humans are starting to be perceived as unique beings when it comes to medication. First research results regarding the utility of medication have come out. One realization is that men and women require different medication and treatment and it is known that Caucasians, in comparison with people of different skin color, require different medication.

We certainly are just at the beginning. However, a first step has at least been made. A growing number of physicians combine the classical methods of treatment with complementary ones.

As you probably have already noticed by the usage of the word „complementary", the habit of thinking in extremes slowly vanishes.

Alternative medicine suggests opposition. Everything will become one great whole in which aspirin, homeopathic medicine, herbal or curd compresses, laying on of hands, singing bowls, light therapy, knocking, and many other things can equally contribute to a successful treatment.

I wish all of us a greater foresight, to be more open for new things, more trust in our culture and a greater understanding of the holistic approach.

In Conclusion

Thank you for being interested! I hope that you had fun reading this book and that it could convey some inspiration and ideas for your own life. The texts collected in this book have given you an insight into my way of thinking and therefore, up to a certain degree, also into my way of working.

You certainly are – just like me – convinced that reading books, especially self-help books, is a wonderful thing. But – according to my motto "Actions speak louder than words!" – you only do something really good for yourself if you cause change as well as live beyond mere reading.

If you would like to change yourself and your life and/or the structures and processes in your company, I am happy to help you with that – as a **consultant and counselor**, as a **seminar leader and behavior coach.** Respect, regard and appreciation are my most important principles for my treatment of and work with people. Integrity, authenticity, honesty, directness, creativity and the ability to give impetus can be seen as my characteristics and strengths.

As a **consultant and counselor,** I can offer you my services as a companion for your individual process of change – no matter what your current "hot topic" is. During the course of our joint work, we will create an action plan that is appropriate for you. The process change counseling within the company is often based on the one-on-one coaching for specialists and executives.

As a **behavior coach,** I have worked with people suffering from obesity within the framework of the OPTIFAST® 52 dietary program. For an entire year, it is my task to mediate to them that they should start taking better care of themselves and I support them in changing their diet in the long run.

My **seminars** are specially tailored to your and your company's needs. You decide the content because you know how your company should work and function and what support you and your employees need. My portfolio includes, among other things, communications coaching for new employees with customer contact or „empowering women" – security training for women, e.g. in communication with male colleagues and in order to ensure that „one understands the language of the other" – gender communication.

Welcome to the new life!

Another reference to my work as a speaker.

I give talks about my motto **"Actions speak louder than words"**. This includes many topics, such as letting go, saying goodbye, dreams, lifestyle analyses, coaching, women, the pitfalls of love, relationship counseling, showboats in the workplace and many other things.

Have you become curious? Then I wholeheartedly welcome you to one of my websites:

My method	www.lisa-methode.de
Publishing house	www.menschin.com
My company	www.cn-counseling.de
Speaker	www.christanehls360.com
XING	www.xing.de/profile/Christa_Nehls
LinkedIn	www.linkedin.com/pub/christa-nehls/20/73/561
Facebook	www.facebook.com/christa.nehls
Twitter	www.twitter.com/ChristaNehls

Contact Information:

Christa Nehls

Consultant & Coach
for specialists and executives
Author & Speaker

Krappmühlstraße 17
68165 Mannheim, Germany

Phone: 0621 44069100
Mobile: 0170 3023302

menschin@menschin.com

www.ingramcontent.com/pod-product-compliance
Lightning Source LLC
Chambersburg PA
CBHW021936160426
43195CB00011B/1111